POPTAILS

Erin Nichols

60 Boozy
Treats Served
on a Stick

Ulysses Press

Published by:
ULYSSES PRESS
P.O. Box 3440
Berkeley, CA 94703
www.ulyssespress.com

ISBN: 978-1-61243-065-2
Library of Congress Catalog Number 2012935760

Printed in China by Everbest through Four Colour Print Group

10 9 8 7 6 5 4 3 2 1

Acquisitions editor: Keith Riegert
Managing editor: Claire Chun
Editors: Alice Riegert, Rebecca Pepper
Proofreader: Lauren Harrison
Interior photographs: © Holland Publishing Inc. except those from shutterstock.com on page 31 © majaan, page 45 © Kosoff, page 66 © Talya, page 69 © de2marco, page 73 © maryo, page 76 © Aleksandr Bryliaev, page 79 © TOSP Photo, page 81 © Liz Van Steenburgh, page 91 © R. MACKAY PHOTOGRAPHY, LLC, page 97 © Palle Christensen, page 101 © Abel Tumik, page 104 © M. Unal Ozmen, page 113 © FunStudio
Cover photograph: © Holland Publishing Inc.
Cover design: what!design @ whatweb.com

Distributed by Publishers Group West

To Gram and Wum

for always looking the other way whenever I made "potions" in the kitchen.

Table of Contents

Introduction

I highly doubt that there was a single day in the summer months of my childhood when I didn't consume at least one Popsicle. Whether in push-pop form, push-up plastic sleeves, or a rainbow of sticky fruit juice frozen into cylindrical shapes on a stick, those icy treats were the perfect antidote to the seemingly endless hot and humid New England days—all six or seven of them.

I kid. It really can get uncomfortably hot in the northeastern United States. Just pour me a glass of wine or two and I'll fill you in on the trials and sweaty tribulations involved in the gigantic mistake I made a few years ago when I rented a swanky loft in a Boston suburb that didn't come with air conditioning. By 7:30 a.m. every day, I strongly resembled Ashley Judd's constantly perspiring character in *A Time to Kill*. As my poor cats and I huddled in front of an array of unsatisfactory fans, the exposed beams and well-appointed kitchen offered little in the way of consolation. Now that was a time when I really could have used an ice pop. Or better yet, an ice pop with a little kick.

Gin and tonics, mimosas, and strawberry-basil martinis are all well and good, but wouldn't it be glorious to tote your favorite cocktail around on the end of a jaunty wooden stick? Everything from grilled cheese to apple pie is plunked onto a sturdy handle these days. Why should your post-work, liquid form of unwinding be any different? Just picture it: pretty pastel peach Bellinis glistening in the sun, a bouquet of cherry-topped Manhattans passed around the living room as a predinner treat, or perhaps a batch of spicy Bloody Marys shaped like rocket ships brought out at brunch to wow your out-of-town guests.

But wait a minute. Right about now you're probably thinking, "That's lovely, Erin, but alcohol doesn't freeze." And you'd of course be correct. In their natural state, liquors like vodka and gin definitely do not turn into booze-sicles when you leave them in your freezer safely ensconced in their glass bottles. Wine does freeze, though, which I learned the hard way when I forgot all about a bottle

that was chilling in my freezer. As the wine froze, the cork was gradually forced right out of the unopened bottle, and a Sauvignon Blanc skating rink opened for business. My frozen spinach and English muffins were ecstatic about the new slippery development. I decidedly was not. But I digress …

To create proper Poptails, we're going to cook most of our liquors just a bit, evaporating off some of the alcohol while retaining the flavor. I doubt your new favorite dessert will ever give you a hangover, but rest assured that the Dirty Martini pop tastes like a dirty martini and the Irish Coffee pop still has a proper amount of whiskey-fueled zing.

A Few Useful Tools to Have on Hand

First things first. Here are a few excellent tools you may want to consider investing in as you venture into your Poptails kitchen adventure. They'll make things infinitely easier for you in the long run and save you oodles of time, hassle, and potential kitchen-related meltdowns.

Kitchen beaker: This clever contraption looks as though it belongs in your high school science lab, and chances are it did accompany you through a half-dozen lab reports back in the day. I think it's so much better than a traditional measuring cup, and I love that it features a huge array of measuring units, from cups to ounces to pints and even milliliters. It's perfect for measuring all of your liquids, pre- and post-preparation, for your pops. My favorite brand is the Emsa Perfect Beaker.

Tovolo popsicle molds: This is the brand that I've used for years, absolutely love, and would highly recommend purchasing for your pop experimentation. They are dishwasher safe, are individually portioned, come with built-in drip guards, and best of all are available in a large assortment of super-cute shapes and styles. This means that your dream of creating tequila sunrise–shaped stars and jewel pop mint mojitos is only a trip to the mall away.

Citrus squeezer/press: An absurd name for sure, but an invaluable cocktail resource. In all of the recipes in this book, I recommend using fresh fruit whenever possible. This is especially true when it comes to the Poptails that feature lemon and lime juice as an ingredient. You can get away with store-bought orange juice in the recipes, but if you squeeze the faux lemon and lime liquid that comes in the little plastic bottles into your ice pops, the result will be revolting. It's much too acidic. You can definitely tell the difference between fresh and faux.

I realize that squeezing ½ cup of fresh lemon juice might take a few minutes, but with the aid of a citrus squeezer or press you'll make short work of the task. Whatever you do, don't try to use a wooden or plastic citrus reamer. I practically gave myself carpal tunnel syndrome one afternoon trying to collect a large amount of fresh lime juice for a mojito party.

Since that day, I've never been without my bright yellow press. Norco and Ampro both make excellent versions of this trusty tool.

Food coloring: One of the best parts about ice pops (aside from that whole icy goodness thing) is the gorgeous array of edible colors and hues that emerge from your freezer. Of course, this is dependent upon your use of ingredients and level of patience, but as we're constantly reminded, we eat with our eyes. To that end, I made an executive decision to add food coloring to a number of the recipes in this book.

There are many very attractive pink, blue, green, and even red liqueurs, but once they're mixed with other ingredients (juices, yogurts, and pudding, to name just a few), you sometimes end up with a bowl of delicious mix that has taken an unfortunate ride on the boring side. So if your orange creamsicle base isn't knocking your socks off, feel free to get a little help from the "coloring box." Beautifying your pops is nothing to be ashamed of, and you'll be much more satisfied with the end results. Tried-and-true McCormick food color and egg dyes are excellent options for pumping up the color in your Poptails.

How to Prepare Alcohol for Use in Your Poptails

Now for the most important step in your boozy pops adventure. We have to prepare the alcohol so it will actually freeze into sweet shapes and colorful layers that will wow your friends and frenemies alike.

The table on page 11 details the approximate amounts of liquor before and after being brought to a boil. The general rule of thumb is that 1 cup of liquor yields approximately ¾ cup of prepared liquor to use in your recipe.

Yes, I really did test this with a wide array of liquors of varying proofs. In fact, I even came up with a hypothesis for my experiment. My college biology professor would have been so proud! After slaving over a hot stovetop with my trusty timer in hand, I found that the level of alcohol proof does not affect the yield significantly when liquors are boiled under identical conditions and for the same amount of time. Or at least it doesn't for the short span that you'll be boiling your liquors for the recipes. Does that sound complicated? It's really not. Just follow the table below to get started.

Amount of Alcohol in Recipe	Add This Much Alcohol to Your Pan
¼ cup	½ cup
½ cup	¾ cup
¾ cup	1 cup
1 cup	1¼ cups
1¼ cups	1½ cups

Now follow the instructions below.

You Will Need

- A heavy-bottomed 2-quart saucepan
- The liquor you intend to use in the recipe
- A timer
- A heatproof bowl or container to store and cool the prepared liquor

I prepare all of my alcohol in a small, heavy-bottomed 2-quart saucepan. Using a different-sized saucepan could potentially affect your prepared yields, so please keep that in mind.

After reviewing the chart, pour the indicated amount of liquor into the saucepan. For instance, if you need ¾ cup of vodka for your recipe, you will add 1 cup of vodka to the pan. Turn the heat to high. Prepare to settle in for the next 5 minutes or so. Don't run off to fold socks or feed the dog. You really do need to keep a careful eye on the alcohol as it heats on the stove.

As soon as the liquid begins to bubble, set your timer for 2 minutes. You do not have to wait until it is frolicking at a rolling boil.

When the timer sounds, remove the pan promptly from the stove. Remember, you're working with a boiling substance, so be careful! Immediately (but with caution) pour the liquid into your heatproof container. Do not leave it in the pan to cool. The pan is super hot, and your yield will be lower if you leave the liquor in the warm pan. Finally, place the liquid in the refrigerator and allow it to cool completely.

Flattening Soda and Other Fizzy Beverages

Any carbonated liquids that you use in your Poptails will need to be flattened. This includes soda pops, tonics, and champagnes. Sorry, friends. There isn't a magic solution to this. I wish that I could wave my glitter-covered wand and cause your bubbly drinks to instantly go still and quiet, so you could make dozens of pops immediately, but that's simply not the case.

I highly recommend opening any containers of champagne, tonic water, club soda, ginger ale, and other sodas at least 8 hours before you plan to work with them. Just to be safe, before going to bed I usually open the bottle and tuck it somewhere where it won't fall over in my refrigerator during the night. You don't want to wake up to find a sticky pool of ginger ale populating the bottom shelf and your asparagus and cold cuts indulging in a sunrise swim. A few bubbles may still be grooving around in your bottle the next morning. That's ok. The goal is to weaken those fizzy beverages as much as possible prior to use, not to force them into complete submission.

You're going to be tempted just to open a can of pop or a bottle of bubbly and use it in the recipes. I can relate. I'm the queen of impatient cooking, but believe me when I say that you don't want to do that. Cleaning champagne and ginger beer icicles out of your freezer is not how you want to spend your afternoon. I've cleaned more than my share of "volcanic" pop eruptions from the freezer due to my personal ice pop impatience, and I really don't think you want to experience this super-fun chore in your own kitchen. If your pops do overflow, don't try to clean up the spill with paper towels, or you'll end up with a frothy paper mess. I've done it all, folks! If you insist, please note that a damp kitchen towel works best.

Making Simple Syrups

Well, party pop people, it doesn't get much easier than this. Simple syrup is a concoction of equal parts sugar and water, which is brought to a boil, cooled, and then added to cocktails in order to make them fantastic. If you're a mojito fan, you probably already have an advanced degree in simple syrup creation. That was the gateway recipe that introduced me to this ingredient. The nice thing about simple syrup is that you can make a little or a lot and then store it in your fridge for weeks. Then, when the mood strikes, you just whip it out and do your thing.

I store my simple syrup in a canning jar these days, but once upon a time I was known to keep it in an old Nalgene water bottle. Imagine the surprise of the poor unsuspecting soul who accidentally took that particular bottle to the gym. Oops!

SIMPLE SYRUP

MAKES 1½ CUPS

1 cup white sugar

1 cup water

1. Combine the sugar and water in a medium saucepan over medium-high heat.

2. While the mixture heats, continue to stir until all of the sugar has been dissolved. Bring the syrup to a boil.

3. Remove the pan from the stovetop and allow the syrup to cool on a heat-safe surface.

4. Pour the syrup into a sealable container and store it in your refrigerator until the Poptail mood strikes, or for up to 1 month.

Simple Syrup Variations

Three recipes in this book call for a variation on the simple syrup recipe. One Poptail features a simple syrup made with brown sugar, another uses a simple syrup infused with fresh ginger, and a third calls for mint-infused syrup. The recipes for these three items follow.

BROWN SUGAR SIMPLE SYRUP

MAKES 1½ CUPS

   1 cup light or dark brown sugar

   1 cup water

1. Combine the brown sugar and water in a medium saucepan over medium-high heat.

2. While the mixture heats, continue to stir until all of the sugar has been dissolved. Bring the syrup to a boil.

3. Remove the pan from the stovetop, and allow the syrup to cool on a heat-safe surface.

4. Pour the syrup into a sealable container and refrigerate.

GINGER-INFUSED SIMPLE SYRUP

MAKES 1½ CUPS

   1 cup white sugar

   1 cup water

   ¼ cup minced fresh ginger

1. Combine the sugar, water, and ginger in a medium saucepan over medium-high heat.

2. While the mixture heats, continue to stir until all of the sugar has been dissolved. Bring the syrup to a boil.

3. Remove the pan from the stovetop and allow the syrup to cool on a heat-safe surface.

4. Pour the syrup through a fine-mesh sieve into a bowl. Discard the ginger.

5. Pour the strained syrup into a sealable container and refrigerate.

MINT-INFUSED SIMPLE SYRUP

MAKES 1½ CUPS

1 cup white sugar

1 cup water

1 cup fresh mint leaves

1. Combine the sugar, water, and mint in a medium saucepan over medium-high heat.

2. While the mixture heats, continue to stir until all of the sugar has been dissolved. Bring the syrup to a boil.

3. Remove the pan from the stovetop and allow the syrup to cool on a heat-safe surface.

4. Pour the syrup through a fine-mesh sieve into a bowl. Discard the mint.

5. Pour the strained syrup into a sealable container and refrigerate.

Removing Pops from Their Molds

After your pops have relaxed in the freezer for at least 24 hours, it's time for them to make a grand appearance. Here are a few tips on how to get them to come out of their shells without oodles of flattery and coaxing.

Note: Each recipe in this book yields six 3-ounce pops or four 4-ounce pops.

For individual pop molds: The most effective way to remove deeply chilled pops from their containers is to run each pop mold carefully under warm running water. Pay special attention to the tip of the pop mold, and be careful not to accidentally pour water into the mold via the opening seams on their tops.

Sometimes you'll need to run pops under warm water for up to a minute. Gently tug on the ice pop stick to test whether or not it will release from the mold. Patience is your best course of action here. Forcing the pops from their molds without first releasing the sides will almost certainly result in broken pops and lots of frowns all around. Rest assured that even the most stubborn pops (usually the ones with fruit puree) will eventually have to give in, pop out into the open, and be eaten.

For one-piece pop mold sets: A warm cup or bowl of water is your best friend in this instance. To remove a single pop from a set of inseparable ice pop molds, place the bottom of the mold into the bowl of warm water. Allow it to sit for 15 seconds, and then gently tug on the top or ice pop stick. If the pop does not release, allow it to warm in the water for 15 more seconds and then check again. Repeat this process until the pop emerges from the plastic mold.

CHAPTER ONE

COLORFUL COCKTAILS

STRAWBERRY-BASIL MARTINI

Although this pop is certainly not a traditional martini, I still think you'll love the fresh taste of tart strawberry and savory basil mixed into cold vodka, with just a hint of lime. If you puree the fruits, the pop will have a pretty speckled look that promises not to clash with your new linen napkins.

1¼ cups prepared vodka (page 10)

16 ounces (1 quart) fresh or thawed frozen strawberries (if using fresh berries, be sure to remove the stems)

⅓ cup packed fresh basil leaves

2 tablespoons freshly squeezed lime juice

1. Prepare and chill the vodka of your choice.

2. Chop the strawberries into ¼-inch pieces. For a smoother pop, place the basil, strawberries, and lime juice in a food processor or blender. Puree until smooth. This should yield approximately 1¼ cups of puree.

3. Combine the chopped strawberries and basil or the fruit puree with the prepared vodka in a medium bowl.

4. Carefully divide the mixture equally among your ice pop molds. Do not fill the molds to the top. Leave a small amount of space to allow for expansion when the liquid freezes.

5. Top with ice pop sticks or reusable ice pop tops with attached sticks. Let the pops freeze for at least 24 hours.

6. To unmold the pops, see page 16.

APPLETINI

Oh, appletini. You are consumed with an air of irony on primetime sitcoms like Scrubs *and* Two and a Half Men, *but once people manage to get past your shocking green color, they find it's really quite easy to enjoy your candylike flavor. This signature cocktail translates perfectly to pop form, with a little help from a few drops of food coloring.*

1 cup prepared vodka (page 10)

¾ cup prepared sour apple schnapps (page 10)

¾ cup flattened tonic water (page 12)

6 drops green food coloring

1. Prepare and chill the vodka and sour apple schnapps, and let the tonic water flatten for at least 8 hours.

2. In a medium bowl, combine the vodka, sour apple schnapps, tonic water, and food coloring.

3. Carefully divide the mixture equally among your ice pop molds. Do not fill the molds to the top. Leave a small amount of space to allow for expansion when the liquid freezes.

4. Top with ice pop sticks or reusable ice pop tops with attached sticks. Let the pops freeze for at least 24 hours.

5. To unmold the pops, see page 16.

LEMON DROP

This sweet-and-sour pop will leave your lips pursed and puckered, but strangely enough you'll still crave more! I'm admittedly not a lemon fan—lemon-flavored candy always gets left behind in my snacking wake. But shake up this fresh citrus flavor in a cocktail glass—or freeze it into a pop—and we're the best of friends.

1 cup prepared limoncello (page 10)

1 cup simple syrup (page 14)

½ cup freshly squeezed lemon juice

1. Prepare and chill the limoncello of your choice and the simple syrup.

2. In a medium bowl, combine the limoncello, simple syrup, and lemon juice.

3. Carefully divide the mixture equally among your ice pop molds. Do not fill the molds to the top. Leave a small amount of space to allow for expansion when the liquid freezes.

4. Top with ice pop sticks or reusable ice pop tops with attached sticks. Let the pops freeze for at least 24 hours.

5. To unmold the pops, see page 16.

COSMOPOLITAN

A quintessential pop-culture cocktail, the cosmopolitan catapulted to stardom via the equally addictive HBO dramedy Sex and the City. *The cosmo is the little pink drink that became the go-to gal pal libation of the oughts. From happy hours to baby showers, it may have jumped the shark a bit in terms of popularity, but I still like to imbibe from time to time and argue with my girlfriends about which one of us is Carrie, Samantha, Charlotte, and Miranda. Don't you think Charlotte would be a huge Poptails fan?*

1 cup prepared vodka (page 10)

⅓ cup prepared triple sec (page 10)

⅓ cup freshly squeezed lime juice

¾ cup cranberry juice

1. Prepare and chill the vodka and triple sec of your choice.
2. In a medium bowl, combine the vodka, triple sec, lime juice, and cranberry juice.
3. Carefully divide the mixture equally among your ice pop molds. Do not fill the molds to the top. Leave a small amount of space to allow for expansion when the liquid freezes.
4. Top with ice pop sticks or reusable ice pop tops with attached sticks. Let the pops freeze for at least 24 hours.
5. To unmold the pops, see page 16.

THE CAPE COD

Charming, pink, and boozy are the three adjectives that come to mind when I think of this quintessentially New England drink. This summer libation simply begs to be translated into ice pop form so it can be tucked away in a cooler with your lobster and taffy and then carried to a private beach party or a sunset sail. I can almost smell the salt-tinged air …

1 cup prepared vodka (page 10)

1¼ cups cranberry juice

¼ cup freshly squeezed lime juice

1. Prepare and chill the vodka of your choice.

2. In a medium bowl, combine the vodka, cranberry juice, and lime juice.

3. Carefully divide the mixture equally among your ice pop molds. Do not fill the molds to the top. Leave a small amount of space to allow for expansion when the liquid freezes.

4. Top with ice pop sticks or reusable ice pop tops with attached sticks. Let the pops freeze for at least 24 hours.

5. To unmold the pops, see page 16.

WHISKEY SOUR

On my 21st birthday, a whiskey sour was the first drink I legally celebrated with, so this pop has a soft spot in my inner (and sometimes very extroverted) party girl heart.

> 1¼ cups prepared whiskey (page 10)
>
> 1¼ cups sour mix
>
> 4 or 6 maraschino cherries (1 for each pop), stems removed

1. Prepare and chill the whiskey of your choice.

2. In a medium bowl, combine the whiskey and sour mix.

3. Carefully divide the mixture equally among your ice pop molds. Do not fill the molds to the top. Leave a small amount of space to allow for expansion when the liquid freezes.

4. Place a single maraschino cherry in each pop mold.

5. Top with ice pop sticks or reusable ice pop tops with attached sticks. Let the pops freeze for at least 24 hours.

6. To unmold the pops, see page 16.

SCREWDRIVER

Simple yet effective, these pops based on the tried-and-true drink develop a slightly more sophisticated edge if you take a few extra minutes to make freshly squeezed orange juice and retire that old "from concentrate" carton to the back of your fridge.

> 1 cup prepared vodka (page 10)
>
> 1½ cups orange juice, preferably freshly squeezed

1. Prepare and chill the vodka of your choice.

2. In a medium bowl, combine the vodka and orange juice.

3. Carefully divide the mixture equally among your ice pop molds. Do not fill the molds to the top. Leave a small amount of space to allow for expansion when the liquid freezes.

4. Top with ice pop sticks or reusable ice pop tops with attached sticks. Let the pops freeze for at least 24 hours.

5. To unmold the pops, see page 16.

MINT JULEP

Mint juleps are synonymous with lazy summer days, over-the-top hats, and horse racing. Much to my chagrin, I've never had the opportunity to sport a ribbon-and-flower-festooned bonnet to a big Triple Crown event, but rest assured, it will happen someday. In the meantime, for those of you who share my hat fetish, I suppose we can just sit in the backyard and pretend we're fashionable Southern folks while enjoying this super-sweet and minty treat.

  1 cup prepared whiskey (page 10)

  1½ cups mint-infused simple syrup (page 16)

  1 tablespoon very finely minced fresh mint, divided

1. Prepare and chill the whiskey of your choice and the mint-infused simple syrup.

2. In a medium bowl, combine the whiskey and mint-infused syrup.

3. Sprinkle half of the finely minced mint into the ice pop molds, dividing it evenly.

4. Carefully divide the liquid mixture equally among the ice pop molds, pouring it over the mint. Do not fill the molds to the top. Leave a small amount of space to allow for expansion when the liquid freezes.

5. Sprinkle the remaining mint into the molds, dividing it evenly, and then top with ice pop sticks or reusable ice pop tops with attached sticks. Let the pops freeze for at least 24 hours.

6. To unmold the pops, see page 16.

CHAPTER TWO

TROPICAL TREATS

BLUE HAWAII

This pop might look like a science experiment once it's frozen, but it certainly doesn't taste like it came from a boring old lab. Bright blue curaçao is mixed with sweet crème de cacao and crushed pineapple pieces to create a blue-green oceanic effect. You'll feel as though you've been transported to an island paradise after the very first taste. Just be sure to keep your eyes peeled for ice-pop–loving sharks.

½ cup prepared vodka (page 10)

½ cup prepared blue curaçao (page 10)

½ cup prepared crème de cacao (page 10)

1 cup crushed canned pineapple, juice included

1. Prepare and chill the vodka, curaçao, and crème de cacao of your choice.

2. In a medium bowl, combine the three alcohols with the crushed pineapple.

3. Carefully divide the mixture equally among your ice pop molds. Do not fill the molds to the top. Leave a small amount of space to allow for expansion when the liquid freezes.

4. Top with ice pop sticks or reusable ice pop tops with attached sticks. Let the pops freeze for at least 24 hours.

5. To unmold the pops, see page 16.

PIÑA COLADA

If I even glance at the words "piña colada," that maddening song slinks into my head and refuses to go away. I've often thought that it's a very good thing piña coladas taste so outlandishly good, or I'd have to boycott them in order to save my sanity from the Jimmy Buffet–induced "earworm" that always takes hold and inevitably leads me to worry that next I'll begin feeling the need to get "caught in the rain."

> 1 cup prepared white rum (page 10)
>
> ½ cup cream of coconut
>
> 1 cup pineapple juice
>
> 4 or 6 maraschino cherries (1 for each pop), stems removed

1. Prepare and chill the white rum of your choice.

2. In a medium bowl, combine the rum, cream of coconut, and pineapple juice.

3. Carefully divide the mixture equally among your ice pop molds. Do not fill the molds to the top. Leave a small amount of space to allow for expansion when the liquid freezes.

4. Add a single maraschino cherry to each mold.

5. Top with ice pop sticks or reusable ice pop tops with attached sticks. Let the pops freeze for at least 24 hours.

6. To unmold the pops, see page 16.

THE DRUNKEN BANANA

I'm fairly certain that I've loved all types of banana-based dishes, candies, and baked goods since birth. These pops feature a super-creamy yogurt base, chunks of fresh fruit, and a nutty touch of amaretto liqueur that creates a seriously addictive combination. You've been warned.

¾ cup prepared amaretto, such as Disaronno (page 10)

1½ cups banana or banana chiffon yogurt

¼ cup finely diced banana, divided

1. Prepare and chill the amaretto of your choice.

2. In a medium bowl, combine the amaretto and banana yogurt.

3. Carefully divide one third of the yogurt mixture evenly among your ice pop molds.

4. Pop a few banana pieces into each mold.

5. Add another third of the yogurt mixture to your molds.

6. Place a second layer of banana bits in each mold.

7. Finally, add the remaining yogurt mixture to the ice pop molds, and top each with the remaining banana bits. Do not fill the molds to the top. Leave a small amount of space to allow for expansion when the liquid freezes.

8. Top with ice pop sticks or reusable ice pop tops with attached sticks. Let the pops freeze for at least 24 hours.

9. To unmold the pops, see page 16.

TEQUILA SUNRISE

To replicate the sensational tropical-sky appearance of the decidedly beach-friendly cocktail on which this pop is based, you'll very slowly trickle a small amount of bright red grenadine syrup into each ice pop mold. As the ruby red liquid mixes with the tequila and orange juice, a layered fiery sunrise will form and, with the aid of your trusty refrigerator, eventually freeze into place.

> 1¼ cups prepared tequila (page 10)
>
> 1¼ cups orange juice, preferably freshly squeezed
>
> 2 to 3 teaspoons grenadine syrup (½ teaspoon for each pop)

1. Prepare and chill the tequila of your choice.

2. In a medium bowl, combine the tequila and orange juice.

3. Carefully divide the mixture equally among your ice pop molds. Do not fill the molds to the top. Leave a small amount of space to allow for expansion when the liquid freezes.

4. Measure out ½ teaspoon of grenadine. Very slowly pour the liquid into one of the ice pop molds. Repeat this step for each pop you're creating. As the grenadine comes into contact with the orange juice and tequila, a layered sunrise effect will appear.

5. Top with ice pop sticks or reusable ice pop tops with attached sticks. Let the pops freeze for at least 24 hours.

6. To unmold the pops, see page 16.

GOOD MORNING, DEAR!

Cocktail meets super-healthy smoothie flavors in this recipe, but I wouldn't recommend snacking on these orange-pineapple-banana pops before your morning workout or marathon commute. I would, however, wholeheartedly encourage you to add them to your brunch menu. Besides, everyone needs an excuse to buy a bottle of banana schnapps at least once in their life.

1 cup prepared banana schnapps, such as 99 Bananas (page 10)

¾ cup pineapple juice

¾ cup orange juice, preferably freshly squeezed

1. Prepare and chill the banana schnapps.
2. In a medium bowl, combine the schnapps, pineapple juice, and orange juice.
3. Carefully divide the mixture equally among your ice pop molds. Do not fill the molds to the top. Leave a small amount of space to allow for expansion when the liquid freezes.
4. Top with ice pop sticks or reusable ice pop tops with attached sticks. Let the pops freeze for at least 24 hours.
5. To unmold the pops, see page 16.

MARGARITA

When I was in college, there was a bar near campus called the Dugout that served fantastic thick-cut onion rings and margaritas by the pint glass. I indulged in countless postclass decompression sessions at that tiny little hole in the wall. To this day I still do a mental double take when I'm served an ice-cold margarita (on the rocks, of course) in a glass of the proper size and shape, and a part of me wonders, "Shouldn't my drink be bigger?"

1 cup prepared tequila (page 10)

¾ cup prepared triple sec (page 10)

¾ cup freshly squeezed lime juice

A sprinkling of kosher salt or other coarse specialty salt for each pop

1. Prepare and chill the tequila and triple sec of your choice.

2. In a medium bowl, combine the tequila, triple sec, and lime juice.

3. Carefully divide the mixture equally among your ice pop molds. Do not fill the molds to the top. Leave a small amount of space to allow for expansion when the liquid freezes, or your freezer may receive an icy margarita bath.

4. Sprinkle a very small amount of kosher salt into each pop.

5. Top with ice pop sticks or reusable ice pop tops with attached sticks. Let the pops freeze for at least 24 hours.

6. To unmold the pops, see page 16.

PRETTY PINK MARGARITA

Readers of my blog erincooks.com know that I have a rather strong affinity for pretty pink things, so I couldn't possibly neglect my roots and miss out on the chance to make a pretty pink ice pop. This tart pop features a flirty concoction of sexy silver tequila, fresh lemon juice, and dainty store-bought pink lemonade that yields a perfectly preppy treat.

¾ cup prepared silver tequila (page 10)

¼ cup prepared triple sec (page 10)

1¼ cups pink lemonade

¼ cup freshly squeezed lemon juice

1. Prepare and chill the silver tequila and triple sec of your choice.

2. In a medium bowl, combine the tequila, triple sec, pink lemonade, and lemon juice.

3. Carefully divide the mixture equally among your ice pop molds. Do not fill the molds to the top. Leave a small amount of space to allow for expansion when the liquid freezes.

4. Top with ice pop sticks or reusable ice pop tops with attached sticks. Let the pops freeze for at least 24 hours.

5. To unmold the pops, see page 16.

MOJITO

Shh … don't tell anyone, but the first mojito I ever had was at the Cheesecake Factory. Don't judge! They actually make a really good cocktail. I don't know anyone who can resist a minty sweet and refreshing glass of white rum spiked with just the right amount of freshly squeezed lime juice. These clear pops may not turn any heads in the beauty department, but they'll certainly turn on your taste buds.

1 cup prepared white or light rum (page 10)

½ cup simple syrup (page 14)

¾ cup flattened club soda (page 12)

10 fresh mint leaves

¼ cup freshly squeezed lime juice

1. Prepare and chill the rum of your choice and the simple syrup, and let the club soda flatten for at least 8 hours.

2. In a medium bowl, combine the rum, simple syrup, club soda, fresh mint, and lime juice.

3. Muddle the mixture with a muddler or a wooden spoon for at least 1 minute.

4. Strain the mixture through a fine-mesh sieve into a clean bowl. Discard the mint leaves.

5. Carefully divide the mixture equally among your ice pop molds. Do not fill the molds to the top. Leave a small amount of space to allow for expansion when the liquid freezes.

6. Top with ice pop sticks or reusable ice pop tops with attached sticks. Let the pops freeze for at least 24 hours.

7. To unmold the pops, see page 16.

CHAPTER THREE

CLASSIC COCKTAILS

GIN AND TONIC

There's nothing like that first icy gin and tonic of the summer season. This is especially true for those of us that reside in New England. When the temperatures begin to inch past 50 degrees, the winter coats go back into storage, and patios with pretty twinkling lights open back up. It seems only right to celebrate the end of another long, snowy winter with a stiff salute to the forthcoming sun- and sand-filled fun.

> 1 cup prepared gin (page 10)
>
> 1¼ cups flattened tonic water (page 12)
>
> ¼ cup freshly squeezed lime juice

1. Prepare and chill the gin of your choice, and let the tonic water flatten for at least 8 hours.

2. In a medium bowl, combine the gin, tonic water, and lime juice.

3. Carefully divide the mixture equally among your ice pop molds. Do not fill the molds to the top. Leave a small amount of space to allow for expansion when the liquid freezes.

4. Top with ice pop sticks or reusable ice pop tops with attached sticks. Let the pops freeze for at least 24 hours.

5. To unmold the pops, see page 16.

VODKA TONIC

If you're not a gin and tonic fan, it's usually because you reside in the vodka and tonic camp. While I'm a card-carrying member of the G&T club, I'd never want to deprive my vodka-loving rivals of a refreshing ice pop version of their go-to drink.

    1 cup prepared vodka (page 10)

    1¼ cups flattened tonic water (page 12)

    ¼ cup freshly squeezed lime juice

1. Prepare and chill the vodka of your choice, and let the tonic water flatten for at least 8 hours.

2. In a medium bowl, combine the vodka, tonic water, and lime juice.

3. Carefully divide the mixture equally among your ice pop molds. Do not fill the molds to the top. Leave a small amount of space to allow for expansion when the liquid freezes.

4. Top with ice pop sticks or reusable ice pop tops with attached sticks. Let the pops freeze for at least 24 hours.

5. To unmold the pops, see page 16.

DIRTY MARTINI

I adore olives and have yet to meet one that I don't like. Just as mothers aren't supposed to have favorite children, I'm probably not supposed to have a favorite recipe, but if you twisted my arm I could quite possibly be persuaded to tell you that this one is mine. The frozen olives may make it a little strange, but if you're a martini drinker, I think you'll find the concept novel.

   1½ cups prepared vodka (page 10)

   ½ cup prepared dry vermouth (page 10)

   ¼ cup olive juice/brine from the jar

   4 or 6 stuffed green olives (1 for each pop), halved

1. Prepare and chill the vodka and vermouth of your choice.

2. In a medium bowl, combine the vodka, vermouth, and olive brine.

3. Place the two halves of a single olive in each mold.

4. Carefully divide the vodka mixture equally among your ice pop molds. Do not fill the molds to the top. Leave a small amount of space to allow for expansion when the liquid freezes.

5. Top with ice pop sticks or reusable ice pop tops with attached sticks. Let the pops freeze for at least 24 hours.

6. To unmold the pops, see page 16.

MOSCOW MULE

Cocktails that contain ginger beer are, hands down, some of my favorite drinks. I love the comforting flavor of this earthy beverage and urge you to find a good-quality ginger beer that you enjoy on its own before mixing in lime and vodka. The flavor of your ginger beer is very important, and they don't all taste the same.

   ¾ cup prepared vodka (page 10)

   1½ cups flattened ginger beer (page 12)

   ¼ cup freshly squeezed lime juice

1. Prepare and chill the vodka of your choice, and let the ginger beer flatten for at least 8 hours.

2. In a medium bowl, combine the vodka, ginger beer, and lime juice.

3. Carefully divide the mixture equally among your ice pop molds. Do not fill the molds to the top. Leave a small amount of space to allow for expansion when the liquid freezes.

4. Top with ice pop sticks or reusable ice pop tops with attached sticks. Let the pops freeze for at least 24 hours.

5. To unmold the pops, see page 16.

DARK AND STORMY

Arr, me mateys! This recipe creates a hazy pop with a crisp and tangy finish. It also makes me want to turn down the lights, get broody and very melancholy, and then tell a long, involved yarn about pirates, sea monsters, unsettled ghosts on the high seas, and buried treasure.

¾ cup prepared dark rum (page 10)

1½ cups flattened ginger beer (page 12)

¼ cup freshly squeezed lime juice

1. Prepare and chill the dark rum of your choice, and let the ginger beer flatten for at least 8 hours.

2. In a medium bowl, combine the rum, ginger beer, and lime juice.

3. Carefully divide the mixture equally among your ice pop molds. Do not fill the molds to the top. Leave a small amount of space to allow for expansion when the liquid freezes.

4. Top with ice pop sticks or reusable ice pop tops with attached sticks. Let the pops freeze for at least 24 hours.

5. To unmold the pops, see page 16.

SWEET MANHATTAN

I developed an appreciation for Manhattans during a nightly cocktail hour with my boyfriend's grandparents in Connecticut. One "Grandpa Kelly" concoction is enough to put you in a very mellow mood. If you don't like to drink Manhattans in a bar, you really won't enjoy this pop. Manhattans are strong, and while this recipe makes a pretty, cherry-studded pop, it may not be as "user friendly" as many of the other recipes.

1½ cups prepared bourbon, preferably Maker's Mark (page 10)

½ cup prepared sweet vermouth, preferably Noilly Prat Red (page 10)

¼ cup cherry juice from the maraschino jar

6 dashes Angostura bitters

4 or 6 maraschino cherries (1 for each pop), stems removed

1. Prepare and chill the bourbon and vermouth of your choice.
2. In a medium bowl, combine the bourbon, vermouth, cherry juice, and bitters.
3. Place a single cherry in each ice pop mold.
4. Carefully divide the bourbon mixture equally among your ice pop molds. Do not fill the molds to the top. Leave a small amount of space to allow for expansion when the liquid freezes.
5. Top with ice pop sticks or reusable ice pop tops with attached sticks. Let the pops freeze for at least 24 hours.
6. To unmold the pops, see page 16.

IRISH COFFEE

I love ending a rich wine- and carbohydrate-soaked meal with a piping hot cup of coffee topped off with a pleasant glug of whiskey, but do you know what's even better? Floating around a pool on a hot day, smelling sunscreen, and sporting big movie-star sunglasses while holding a frozen version securely on a stick. Hold the mug please!

1 cup prepared Irish whiskey (page 10)

1¼ cups warm freshly brewed strong coffee (warm coffee will allow the brown sugar to melt)

1 tablespoon brown sugar

¼ cup heavy cream

1. Prepare the Irish whiskey of your choice.

2. In a small bowl, combine the warm coffee and sugar. Allow the mixture to cool.

3. In a medium bowl, combine the whiskey, the coffee and sugar mixture, and the heavy cream.

4. Carefully divide the mixture equally among your ice pop molds. Do not fill the molds to the top. Leave a small amount of space to allow for expansion when the liquid freezes.

5. Top with ice pop sticks or reusable ice pop tops with attached sticks. Let the pops freeze for at least 24 hours.

6. To unmold the pops, see page 16.

BLOODY MARY

When I first tried this pop I couldn't believe how tasty spicy tomato juice and a host of other savory ingredients and spices were frozen.

¾ cup prepared vodka (page 10)

1½ cups tomato juice or V8 juice

¼ cup freshly squeezed lemon juice

½ teaspoon Worcestershire sauce

½ teaspoon Tabasco sauce

½ teaspoon sea salt or kosher salt

½ teaspoon freshly ground black pepper

Optional: ¼ cup very finely minced celery

1. Prepare and chill the vodka of your choice.

2. In a medium bowl, combine the vodka, tomato juice, lemon juice, Worcestershire sauce, Tabasco sauce, salt, and pepper.

3. Carefully divide the mixture equally among your ice pop molds. If you are using the minced celery as a garnish, distribute it evenly among the pops at this time. Do not fill the molds to the top. Leave a small amount of space to allow for expansion when the liquid freezes.

4. Top with ice pop sticks or reusable ice pop tops with attached sticks. Let the pops freeze for at least 24 hours.

5. To unmold the pops, see page 16.

CHAPTER FOUR

FIZZIES AND WINE

BELLINI

Bellinis seem impossibly elegant, and they're the perfect accompaniment to a brunch or lazy Sunday afternoon. Their festive color can be altered in an endless rainbow of ways via your choice of fruit. These pops are an effervescent indulgence that will surely put a smile on your guests' faces.

> 1¼ cups flattened prosecco or other sparkling white wine (page 12)
>
> 20 ounces fresh or thawed frozen fruit (peach is traditional, but you can also use raspberry, strawberry, mango, etc.)

1. You do not need to prepare the prosecco or sparkling white wine, but you do need to let it flatten for at least 8 hours.

2. If you prefer a smoother ice pop, puree the fruit in a blender or food processor until smooth. At this point, if the fruit contain seeds, I like to strain the puree through a fine-mesh sieve into a clean bowl and then discard the seeds, but that is entirely optional.

3. In a medium bowl, combine the prosecco and the fruit or fruit puree.

4. Carefully divide the mixture equally among your ice pop molds. Do not fill the molds to the top. Leave a small amount of space to allow for expansion when the liquid freezes.

5. Top with ice pop sticks or reusable ice pop tops with attached sticks. Let the pops freeze for at least 24 hours.

6. To unmold the pops, see page 16.

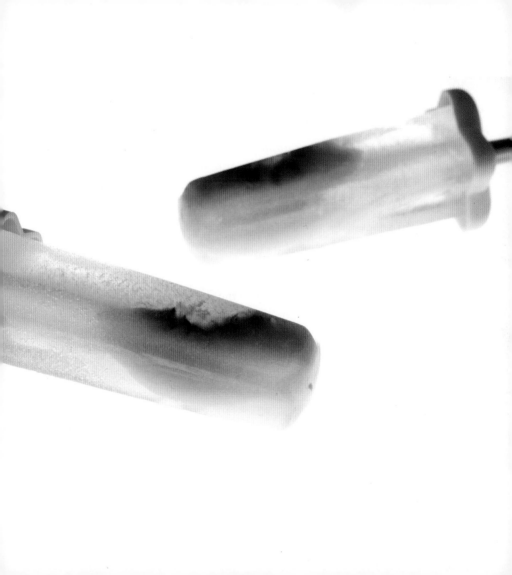

WHITE WINE SPRITZER

These days, white wine spritzers seem relegated to reruns of movies and television shows from the '80s. It entertainingly feels like the kind of drink you should order only if your name happens to be Bunny, you use half a can of Aqua Net on your crimped hair, and you're sporting a white linen suit with big shoulder pads. But perhaps this out-of-fashion little drink deserves a second chance in frozen form?

1¼ cups flattened club soda (page 12)

1¼ cups of your favorite white wine

1. Let the club soda flatten for 8 hours. You do not need to prepare the wine. Simply combine your favorite white wine with the flattened club soda in a medium bowl.

2. Carefully divide the mixture equally among your ice pop molds. Do not fill the molds to the top. Leave a small amount of space to allow for expansion when the liquid freezes.

3. Top with ice pop sticks or reusable ice pop tops with attached sticks. Let the pops freeze for at least 24 hours.

4. To unmold the pops, see page 16.

GINGER FIZZ FIZZ

Please be sure to flatten the champagne in this recipe so that you don't end up with a great big messy surprise when you open your freezer the next day. Champagne icicles might sound appealing, but when you find yourself cleaning them off bags of frozen peas and chipping them away from containers of leftover lasagna, you'll definitely change your tune.

    1 cup ginger-infused simple syrup (page 15)

    1¼ cups flattened champagne (page 12)

    1 tablespoon finely chopped candied ginger

1. Prepare and chill the simple syrup, and let the champagne flatten for at least 8 hours.

2. In a medium bowl, combine the champagne and ginger simple syrup.

3. Carefully divide the mixture equally among your ice pop molds. Do not fill the molds to the top. Leave a small amount of space to allow for expansion when the liquid freezes.

4. At this point, evenly distribute the finely chopped candied ginger among the pops.

5. Top with ice pop sticks or reusable ice pop tops with attached sticks. Let the pops freeze for at least 24 hours.

6. To unmold the pops, see page 16.

WHITE WINE SANGRIA

The fruits listed here are simply suggestions. Feel free to gather your favorites. I'm a sucker for gorgeous pinks and greens, but if you're more of a lemon, pear, and blueberry person, then by all means feel free to substitute. White wine sangria is the quintessential summer drink, so I like to make mine with a summery wine. A sweet yet crisp Sauvignon Blanc usually works nicely.

> 1 cup flattened seltzer water (page 12)
>
> 1 cup white wine
>
> 2 tablespoons finely diced green apple
>
> 2 tablespoons finely diced strawberries
>
> 12 raspberries, halved

1. Let the seltzer water flatten for at least 8 hours. You do not need to prepare the wine. Simply combine the flattened seltzer and white wine in a medium bowl.

2. Place a few pieces of fruit in the bottom of each ice pop mold.

3. Carefully divide the wine and seltzer mixture equally among your ice pop molds. Do not fill the molds to the top. Leave a small amount of space to allow for expansion when the liquid freezes.

4. Divide the remaining fruit evenly among the molds, being sure to alternate the fruit types. This will create a varied and thoroughly mixed pop once frozen.

5. Top with ice pop sticks or reusable ice pop tops with attached sticks. Let the pops freeze for at least 24 hours.

6. To unmold the pops, see page 16.

RED WINE SANGRIA

If you'd like your sangria to be even sweeter, simply squeeze a little citrus juice directly from the unused portion of the fruit into your red wine and seltzer mixture.

1 cup flattened seltzer water (page 12)

1 cup red wine (Cabernet Sauvignon is my favorite)

2 tablespoons finely diced red apple

2 tablespoons finely diced orange segments (peel removed)

2 tablespoons finely diced lemon segments (peel removed)

1. Let the seltzer water flatten for at least 8 hours. You do not need to prepare the wine.

2. Combine the red wine and seltzer in a medium bowl.

3. Place a few pieces of fruit in the bottom of each ice pop mold.

4. Carefully divide the wine and seltzer mixture equally among your ice pop molds. Do not fill the molds to the top. Leave a small amount of space to allow for expansion when the liquid freezes.

5. Divide the remaining fruit evenly among the molds, being sure to alternate the fruit types. This will create a varied and thoroughly mixed pop once frozen.

6. Top with ice pop sticks or reusable ice pop tops with attached sticks. Let the pops freeze for at least 24 hours.

7. To unmold the pops, see page 16.

MULLED WINE

This mixture of red wine, spices, honey, and tangerine will make your house smell like a Christmas fantasy as it bubbles away on the stovetop. Don't be surprised if a neighborly elf or two knocks on your door to see what all the fuss is about. The resulting deep red pop spiked with the homey tastes of citrus, cinnamon, and cloves will have you bursting into carols and wanting to deck the halls, even if you're whipping a batch up in the middle of a July heat wave.

2½ cups red wine (I usually use Cabernet Sauvignon, but use a wine you like to drink)

¼ cup honey

1 cinnamon stick

4 whole cloves

4 allspice berries

2 small tangerines, unpeeled, halved

1. You do not need to prepare the wine. Combine the red wine, honey, cinnamon stick, cloves, and allspice in a medium pot.

2. Squeeze the juice from the tangerines into the red wine mixture and toss all 4 halves into the liquid as well.

3. Bring the liquid to a boil over medium-high heat. Reduce the heat to low and allow the mulled wine to simmer for 10 minutes.

4. Remove from the stove and strain the mixture through a fine-mesh sieve into a clean bowl. Discard the spices and citrus rind.

5. Allow the mixture to cool. Carefully divide the mixture equally among your ice pop molds. Do not fill the molds to the top. Leave a small amount of space to allow for expansion when the liquid freezes.

6. Top with ice pop sticks or reusable ice pop tops with attached sticks. Let the pops freeze for at least 24 hours.

7. To unmold the pops, see page 16.

CHAPTER FIVE

FRUITY REFRESHERS

TRIPLE BERRY THREAT

This is one of the more time-consuming pops in this book. Your food processor will also get quite the workout while prepping the ingredients for this recipe. Although being tied to your kitchen timer while waiting for each of the fruity layers to freeze might feel like an imposition, as the saying goes, good things come to those who wait. These spiked triple-berry pops will yield an elegant outcome worthy of your time and efforts.

¾ cup prepared vodka (page 10), divided

½ cup blueberry puree

½ cup raspberry puree

½ cup strawberry puree

3 tablespoons freshly squeezed lemon juice, divided

1. Prepare and chill the vodka of your choice.

2. In three separate small bowls, combine a single berry puree, ¼ cup of the vodka, and 1 tablespoon of the lemon juice.

3. You will be making three layers of flavor. Begin by carefully dividing one bowl of the berry mixture equally among your ice pop molds, so that each mold is one-third full.

4. Place the partially filled pops in the freezer. Do not add ice pop sticks or tops yet. Allow the pops to freeze for 1 hour.

5. Remove the pops from the freezer and divide the next berry mixture equally among the molds. Freeze again for 1 hour.

6. Finally, top the pops with the third berry puree. Do not fill the molds to the top. Leave a small amount of space to allow for expansion when the liquid freezes.

7. Top with ice pop sticks or reusable ice pop tops with attached sticks and let the pops freeze for at least an additional 24 hours.

8. To unmold the pops, see page 16.

RASPBERRY-LEMON CHA CHA

All I can think about when I drink limoncello these days is the surreal interview that actor Danny DeVito gave on The View *after an evening of supposed late-night drinking with George Clooney. While we probably won't ever get to spend an evening on the town sipping summery potions with a famous movie star, we can still give our own entertaining more pizzazz with a batch of these tangy and tart treats.*

½ cup prepared limoncello (page 10)

½ cup prepared raspberry vodka (page 10)

¾ cup simple syrup (page 14), divided

¼ cup freshly squeezed lemon juice

½ cup raspberry puree

1. Prepare and chill the limoncello and raspberry vodka of your choice and the simple syrup.

2. In a small bowl, combine the limoncello, ½ cup of the simple syrup, and the lemon juice. In a second small bowl, combine the raspberry vodka, remaining ¼ cup simple syrup, and raspberry puree.

3. You'll be making four layers in this recipe. To do so, carefully pour some of the lemon-flavored mixture into your ice pop molds, filling each almost one-fourth full.

4. Place the partially filled pops in the freezer. Do not add ice pop sticks or tops yet. Allow the pops to freeze for 30 minutes.

5. Remove the pops from the freezer and pour the raspberry-flavored mixture into the molds until they are half full. Allow the pops to freeze for 30 additional minutes.

6. Remove the pops from the freezer and pour the remaining lemon-flavored mixture into your container until the molds are three-fourths full. Allow the pops to freeze for 30 additional minutes.

7. Finally, remove the pops from your freezer and pour the raspberry-flavored mixture into the molds until the pops are almost full. Do not fill the molds to the top. Leave a small amount of space to allow for expansion when the liquid freezes.

8. Top your ice pop molds with ice pop sticks and let the pops freeze for at least 24 additional hours.

9. To unmold the pops, see page 16.

BLUEBERRIES FOR GROWN-UP SAL

Since I grew up in Maine, it's only appropriate that I give a shout-out to one of our quintessential storybook divas. Of course Sal, from Robert McCloskey's much-loved picture book Blueberries for Sal, *will forever remain a darling little girl, but I like to imagine that Sal grew up, perhaps studied to be a pastry chef, and now specializes in creating blueberry-centric cuisine at her own bakery lovingly named "Kuplink, Kuplank, Kuplunk" after the whimsical sounds her berries once made as they fell into her trusty tin pail.*

　　1 cup prepared vanilla vodka (page 10)

　　½ cup simple syrup (page 14)

　　1 cup blueberry puree

1. Prepare and chill the vanilla vodka of your choice and the simple syrup.

2. In a medium bowl, combine the vanilla vodka, simple syrup, and blueberry puree.

3. Carefully divide the mixture equally among your ice pop molds. Do not fill the molds to the top. Leave a small amount of space to allow for expansion when the liquid freezes.

4. Top with ice pop sticks or reusable ice pop tops with attached sticks. Let the pops freeze for at least 24 hours.

5. To unmold the pops, see page 16.

THE FRUIT LOOP

A pop inspired by a breakfast cereal? Why not? Fruity, pastel-colored yogurts are mixed with smooth vanilla vodka and then layered for an eye-catching rainbow effect. Since I like my pops to be loud, rather than polite, I encourage you to add a touch of food coloring to each of the three pop mixtures to create a bolder color palette. Hopefully, Toucan Sam won't pay your backyard a visit while you're sampling. If he does, I can't take responsibility for his actions.

> 1 cup prepared vanilla vodka (page 10), divided, or ⅓ cup each prepared cherry, lemon, and lime vodka
>
> ½ cup cherry yogurt
>
> ½ cup lemon or lemon chiffon yogurt
>
> ½ cup key lime yogurt
>
> Optional: Red, green, and yellow food coloring

1. Prepare and chill the vodka(s) of your choice.

2. In three separate small bowls, combine one flavor of yogurt and ⅓ cup prepared vodka. For more vibrantly colored pops, add 3 drops of red, yellow, or green food coloring (red in the cherry mixture, green in the lime mixture, and yellow in the lemon mixture).

3. You will be making three layers of flavor. Begin by carefully dividing one bowl of the yogurt mixture equally among your ice pop molds.

4. Place the partially filled pops in the freezer. Do not add ice pop sticks or tops yet. Freeze the pops for 1 hour.

5. Remove the pops from the freezer and add the second yogurt mixture. Freeze them again for 1 hour.

6. Finally, top the pops with the third yogurt mixture. Do not fill the molds to the top. Leave a small amount of space to allow for expansion when the liquid freezes.

7. Top with ice pop sticks or reusable ice pop tops with attached sticks. Let the pops freeze for at least an additional 24 hours.

8. To unmold the pops, see page 16.

RED, WHITE, AND BLUE

This patriotic layered pop is the perfect accompaniment to Fourth of July fireworks, sparklers, and backyard barbecues. While making these festive desserts, I found that using the crème de cacao and heavy cream layer last in the freezing process makes the other colors much less likely to bleed into one another. When the white mixture is in the middle it can end up with tie-dyed streaks, and somehow I doubt our founding fathers were into the hippie chic look.

⅓ cup prepared raspberry vodka (page 10)

⅓ cup prepared blueberry vodka (page 10)

⅓ cup prepared white crème de cacao (page 10)

½ cup raspberry puree

½ cup blueberry puree

½ cup heavy cream

1. Prepare and chill the raspberry and blueberry vodkas and the white crème de cacao of your choice.

2. Using three separate small bowls, combine the raspberry vodka and raspberry puree in one bowl, the blueberry vodka and blueberry puree in another, and the crème de cacao and heavy cream in the third.

3. You will be making three layers of flavor. Begin by carefully pouring or spooning the raspberry mixture into your ice pop molds, dividing it evenly.

4. Place the partially filled pops in the freezer. Do not add ice pop sticks or tops yet. Allow the pops to freeze for 90 minutes.

5. Remove the pops from the freezer and pour in the blueberry mixture. Freeze them again for 90 minutes.

6. Finally, pour in the white mixture. Do not fill the molds to the top. Leave a small amount of space to allow for expansion when the liquid freezes.

7. Top with ice pop sticks or reusable ice pop tops with attached sticks. Let the pops freeze for at least an additional 24 hours.

8. To unmold the pops, see page 16.

WICKED WATERMELON

I don't think watermelon is used in drink recipes nearly enough. It has so many good things going for it: It's refreshing, it's pink, and it's good for you. We tend to forget this last point. Since watermelon is usually paraded out with the potato chips and onion dip at summer outings, it seems to get lumped in with the junk food crew, but in reality this thirst-quenching fruit is full of antioxidants and an excellent source of vitamins C and A.

> 1 cup prepared watermelon liqueur, such as Watermelon Pucker (page 10)
>
> ½ cup simple syrup (page 14)
>
> 1 cup watermelon puree from a seedless melon

1. Prepare and chill the watermelon liqueur and the simple syrup.

2. In a medium bowl, combine the watermelon liqueur, simple syrup, and watermelon puree.

3. Carefully divide the mixture equally among your ice pop molds. Do not fill the molds to the top. Leave a small amount of space to allow for expansion when the liquid freezes.

4. Top with ice pop sticks or reusable ice pop tops with attached sticks. Let the pops freeze for at least 24 hours.

5. To unmold the pops, see page 16.

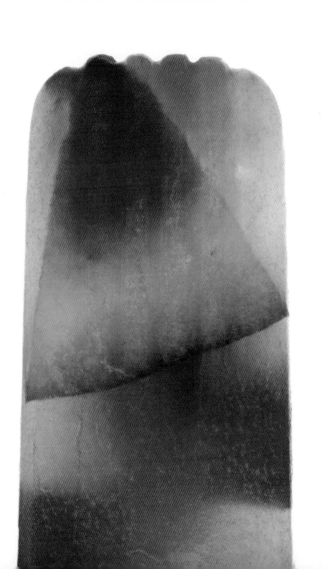

A PROPER GARDEN PARTY

Cucumber sandwiches with the crust cut off, a spicy tomato tart, and a fresh carrot slaw would probably all make a command appearance at a proper sun-filled garden party, but I propose that, instead of slaving in the kitchen all day, you combine the essence of all three in this savory drink and leave the white linen in the closet. No one has the time to iron it anyway.

   ¾ cup prepared cucumber vodka (page 10)

   1 cup carrot juice

   ¾ cup tomato juice

   ½ teaspoon Tabasco sauce

1. Prepare and chill the cucumber vodka of your choice.

2. In a medium bowl, combine the cucumber vodka, carrot juice, tomato juice, and Tabasco sauce.

3. Carefully divide the mixture equally among your ice pop molds. Do not fill the molds to the top. Leave a small amount of space to allow for expansion when the liquid freezes.

4. Top with ice pop sticks or reusable ice pop tops with attached sticks. Let the pops freeze for at least 24 hours.

5. To unmold the pops, see page 16.

THE POM-POM

For a few weeks one winter I was thoroughly seduced by containers of prepped pomegranate seeds that were available at the grocery store. I completely forgot how much fun I have tearing apart and coaxing out the enchanting red pearls from the fruit. Then I realized how much I was spending on those so-called convenient seeds and went back to the old way of doing things. It's infinitely more satisfying, especially if you can use some of your uncovered booty in a blueberry- and vodka-infused pop.

   ¾ cup prepared blueberry vodka (page 10)

   1½ cups pomegranate-blueberry juice

   ¼ cup pomegranate seeds

1. Prepare and chill the blueberry vodka of your choice.

2. In a medium bowl, combine the blueberry vodka and pomegranate-blueberry juice.

3. Carefully divide the mixture equally among your ice pop molds. Do not fill the molds to the top. Leave a small amount of space to allow for expansion when the liquid freezes.

4. Sprinkle the pomegranate seeds into the pops, dividing them evenly.

5. Top with ice pop sticks or reusable ice pop tops with attached sticks. Let the pops freeze for at least 24 hours.

6. To unmold the pops, see page 16.

CHAPTER SIX

PARTY DRINKS

FESTIVE SPIKED EGGNOG

These red and green pops are sure to please Santa himself. At the very least, Mrs. Claus will give you lots of props.

    ¾ cup prepared spiced rum (page 10)

    1¾ cups eggnog (storebought or your favorite family recipe)

    6 drops red food coloring

    6 drops green food coloring

1. Prepare and chill the spiced rum of your choice.

2. In a medium bowl, combine the spiced rum and eggnog.

3. Divide the mixture evenly between two clean bowls. Add 6 drops of red food coloring to one bowl and 6 drops of green food coloring to the other.

4. You will be making two layers. Begin by carefully dividing the red-tinted mixture equally among your ice pop molds so that the molds are almost half full.

5. Place the partially filled pops in your freezer. Do not add ice pop sticks or tops yet. Allow the pops to freeze for 1 hour.

6. Remove the pops from the freezer and divide the green-tinted mixture equally among the molds. Do not fill the molds to the top. Leave a small amount of space to allow for expansion when the liquid freezes.

7. Top with ice pop sticks or reusable ice pop tops with attached sticks. Let the pops freeze for at least an additional 24 hours.

8. To unmold the pops, see page 16.

CHRISTMAS CHEER

I know what you're thinking. Peppermint and eggnog? That just can't work. Promise me you'll try this, though, before you pass persnickety judgment on my taste level. In reality, it's fantastic, and the instructions for layering produce candy cane stripes that make a particularly handsome pop to add to your holiday party menu.

¾ cup prepared peppermint schnapps (page 10)

1¾ cups eggnog (storebought or your favorite family recipe)

6 drops red food coloring

1. Prepare and chill the peppermint schnapps of your choice.

2. In a medium bowl, combine the peppermint schnapps and eggnog.

3. Divide the mixture evenly between two bowls. Add 6 drops of red food coloring to one bowl, and leave the second bowl untinted.

4. You will be making four layers. Begin by carefully pouring some of the red-tinted mixture into your ice pop molds, filling each almost one-fourth full.

5. Place the partially filled pops in your freezer. Do not add ice pop sticks or tops yet. Allow the pops to freeze for 30 minutes.

6. Remove the pops from the freezer and pour some of the untinted mixture into the molds until each is half full. Allow the pops to freeze for 30 more minutes.

7. Next, divide the remaining red-tinted mixture equally among your ice pop molds, so that they are three-fourths full. Freeze the pops again for 30 minutes.

8. Finally, pour the remaining untinted mixture into the molds until each is almost full. Do not fill the molds to the top. Leave a small amount of space to allow for expansion when the liquid freezes.

9. Top with ice pop sticks or reusable ice pop tops with attached sticks. Let the pops freeze for at least 24 hours.

10. To unmold the pops, see page 16.

SPIKED MAPLE-APPLE CIDER

Where I grew up, there was a series of winter events known as Maine Maple Sundays. Essentially, you got to trudge in the cold, through snow and sometimes mud, to little buildings on various farms where sap was being cooked into maple syrup. Next time I get roped into visiting one of these establishments, I'm going to suggest they hand these pops out to the grown-ups. I'm sure it would boost morale significantly.

1 cup prepared whiskey (page 10)

1¼ cups apple cider

¼ cup real maple syrup

1. Prepare and chill the whiskey of your choice.

2. In a medium bowl, combine the whiskey, apple cider, and maple syrup.

3. Carefully divide the mixture equally among your ice pop molds. Do not fill the molds to the top. Leave a small amount of space to allow for expansion when the liquid freezes.

4. Top with ice pop sticks or reusable ice pop tops with attached sticks. Let the pops freeze for at least 24 hours.

5. To unmold the pops, see page 16.

BABY IT'S COLD OUTSIDE

I get so miffed during the holidays when people start spouting nonsense, implying that there's something untoward about the lyrics and goings-on in one of my favorite festive songs. Instead, let's embrace this crooner classic by bundling up properly and making a chilled-down version of a cocoa hot toddy spiked with warm cinnamon and smooth vanilla vodka.

¾ cup prepared vanilla vodka (page 10)

1¾ cups hot cocoa, cooled to room temperature

1 teaspoon ground cinnamon

1. Prepare and chill the vanilla vodka of your choice.

2. In a medium bowl, combine the vanilla vodka, cooled cocoa, and cinnamon.

3. Carefully divide the mixture equally among your ice pop molds. Do not fill the molds to the top. Leave a small amount of space to allow for expansion when the liquid freezes.

4. Top with ice pop sticks or reusable ice pop tops with attached sticks. Let the pops freeze for at least 24 hours.

5. To unmold the pops, see page 16.

GINGER-LEMON ICED TEA

Ah. Iced tea. The drink we all order during working lunches while wishing someone would have the courage to ask the waitress for a great big, shiny margarita. Since that's probably never going to happen, we wait for the weekend and reward ourselves by taking a ho-hum drink to an entirely new level with this concoction of white tea, ginger-flavored spirits, and fresh lemon juice.

¾ cup prepared ginger vodka (page 10)

1½ cups chilled white tea (storebought or brewed at home)

¼ cup freshly squeezed lemon juice

1. Prepare and chill the ginger vodka of your choice.

2. In a medium bowl, combine the ginger vodka, white tea, and lemon juice.

3. Carefully divide the mixture equally among your ice pop molds. Do not fill the molds to the top. Leave a small amount of space to allow for expansion when the liquid freezes.

4. Top with ice pop sticks or reusable ice pop tops with attached sticks. Let the pops freeze for at least 24 hours.

5. To unmold the pops, see page 16.

THE SHIRLEY TEMPLE TANTRUM

I know I wasn't the only little girl who couldn't wait to go out for dinner with her parents (usually Chinese food) so she could order one of these rocking red, fizzy, alcohol-free drinks, pretend she was a sophisticated lady, and then dismantle the flashy paper umbrella that garnished it. Since reminiscing is always easier if something 80-proof is involved, these Shirley Temples are soaked with coordinating raspberry vodka for a frozen bit of spiked nostalgia.

> ¾ cup prepared raspberry vodka (page 10)
>
> 1¾ cups flattened ginger ale (page 12)
>
> 2 tablespoons grenadine syrup

1. Prepare and chill the raspberry vodka of your choice, and let the ginger ale flatten for at least 8 hours.
2. In a medium bowl, combine the raspberry vodka, ginger ale, and grenadine.
3. Carefully divide the mixture equally among your ice pop molds. Do not fill the molds to the top. Leave a small amount of space to allow for expansion when the liquid freezes.

4. Top with ice pop sticks or reusable ice pop tops with attached sticks. Let the pops freeze for at least 24 hours.

5. To unmold the pops, see page 16.

CHAPTER SEVEN

PUDDING
AND CREAM

CHOCOLATE-RASPBERRY PUDDING PATCH

My grandmother had a large raspberry patch that grew right outside her bedroom window. I used to love it when she'd give me a small tin cup (yes, just like Laura Ingalls) and send me out to pick berries for a treat. I always tried to find the plumpest, most brightly colored fruit on the bushes, so my cup would be absolutely perfect. Plump berries play a major role in this frozen treat as well, as they're layered between rich chocolate pudding and raspberry liqueur that yields a tangy frozen surprise with each lick.

¾ cup prepared raspberry liqueur, such as Chambord (page 10)

1½ cups chocolate pudding

12 to 18 plump fresh raspberries (3 for each pop)

1. Prepare and chill the raspberry liqueur of your choice.

2. In a medium bowl, combine the raspberry liqueur and chocolate pudding.

3. Carefully spoon one third of the pudding mixture into your ice pop molds, dividing it evenly.

4. Pop 1 raspberry into each mold.

5. Add another third of the pudding mixture to your molds.

6. Pop 1 more raspberry in each mold.

7. Finally, add the remaining pudding mixture and top each pop with a final raspberry. Do not fill the molds to the top. Leave a small amount of space to allow for expansion when the liquid freezes.

8. Top with ice pop sticks or reusable ice pop tops with attached sticks. Let the pops freeze for at least 24 hours.

9. To unmold the pops, see page 16.

THE NEAPOLITAN

I was that kid. The one who would eat all of the chocolate ice cream from the Neapolitan container, followed by the vanilla, and then leave the strawberry all cold and alone in the back of the freezer. To make up for my past wrongdoings, I've decided to allow strawberry a chance to redeem itself via this striking layered pop made from ingredients you might already have around the house. If you harbor similar strawberry-flavored doubts, just make sure it's the top layer. One quick bite and you'll be in chocolate territory.

> 1 cup prepared vanilla vodka (page 10), divided, or ⅓ cup each prepared chocolate, vanilla, and strawberry vodka
>
> ½ cup chocolate milk
>
> ½ cup white chocolate or vanilla milk
>
> ½ cup strawberry milk

1. Prepare and chill the vodka(s) of your choice.

2. In three separate small bowls, combine one flavor of milk and ⅓ cup vodka (matching the flavors if you use flavored vodkas).

3. You will be making three layers of flavor. Begin by carefully pouring one of the mixtures into your ice pop molds, dividing it evenly.

4. Place the partially filled pops in the freezer. Do not add ice pop sticks or tops yet. Allow the pops to freeze for 1 hour.

5. Remove the pops from the freezer and pour in the second mixture. Freeze them again for 1 hour.

6. Finally, top the pops with the third mixture. Do not fill the molds to the top. Leave a small amount of space to allow for expansion when the liquid freezes.

7. Top with ice pop sticks or reusable ice pop tops with attached sticks. Let the pops freeze for at least an additional 24 hours.

8. To unmold the pops, see page 16.

WHITE RUSSIAN

"Nobody calls me Lebowski. You got the wrong guy. I'm the dude, man."
With that line of dialogue, actor Jeff Bridges, who played a lovable, White
Russian–swilling loser in The Big Lebowski, *became forever recognizable*
as "the Dude," and an entire generation of moviegoers began to associate
his signature concoction of vodka, coffee liqueur, and half-and-half with
bowling and very shabby sweaters.

1¼ cups prepared vodka (page 10)

½ cup prepared coffee liqueur, such as Kahlúa (page 10)

¾ cup half-and-half

1. Prepare and chill the vodka and coffee liqueur of your choice.

2. In a medium bowl, combine the vodka and coffee liqueur with the half-and-half.

3. Carefully divide the mixture equally among your ice pop molds. Do not fill the molds to the top. Leave a small amount of space to allow for expansion when the liquid freezes.

4. Top with ice pop sticks or reusable ice pop tops with attached sticks. Let the pops freeze for at least 24 hours.

5. To unmold the pops, see page 16.

THE PRIMARY SCHOOL PEAR

I had to use food coloring when I made these. I simply couldn't reconcile the elegant starkness of this seemingly naked pear pudding pop with the glaring green cartoon image of the fruit that exists in my head, so I found it necessary to meld the two. You're welcome to skip the food coloring, but I will continue to keep my unrealistic primary school color sensibilities intact.

> 1 cup prepared pear vodka (page 10)
>
> 1½ cups French vanilla or white chocolate pudding
>
> Optional: 6 drops green food coloring

1. Prepare and chill the pear vodka of your choice.

2. In a medium bowl, combine the pear vodka and pudding, adding green food coloring if you like.

3. Carefully divide the mixture equally among your ice pop molds. Do not fill the molds to the top. Leave a small amount of space to allow for expansion when the liquid freezes.

4. Top with ice pop sticks or reusable ice pop tops with attached sticks. Let the pops freeze for at least 24 hours.

5. To unmold the pops, see page 16.

THE HIGHBROW PEAR

The flavor combo in this pop is drop-dead delicious. The nuttiness of the amaretto combined with fresh pear puree and silky chocolate makes you feel as though you're eating something much more highbrow than a pudding pop. Don't let the unassuming exterior fool you. This pop is in it to win it.

¾ cup prepared amaretto liqueur, such as Disaronno (page 10)

1 cup pear puree (if using fresh pears, make sure to peel them before pureeing the fruit)

¾ cup chocolate pudding

1. Prepare and chill the amaretto of your choice.

2. In a medium bowl, combine the amaretto, pear puree, and chocolate pudding.

3. Carefully divide the mixture equally among your ice pop molds. Do not fill the molds to the top. Leave a small amount of space to allow for expansion when the liquid freezes.

4. Top with ice pop sticks or reusable ice pop tops with attached sticks. Let the pops freeze for at least 24 hours.

5. To unmold the pops, see page 16.

CHERRY CORDIAL

My aim with this pop was to create a treat that tastes like the chocolate-covered cherries that seem to appear on every single display that bedecks the big box stores throughout the Christmas season. They also tend to make a command appearance at workplace Yankee Swap events, which is where I was finally coaxed into eating them after shunning them throughout my childhood.

¾ cup prepared cherry vodka (page 10)

¾ cup chocolate pudding

¾ cup cherry-flavored yogurt

12 maraschino cherries, quartered

1. Prepare and chill the cherry vodka of your choice.

2. In a medium bowl, combine the cherry vodka, chocolate pudding, cherry yogurt, and maraschino cherries.

3. Carefully divide the mixture equally among your ice pop molds. Do not fill the molds to the top. Leave a small amount of space to allow for expansion when the liquid freezes.

4. Top with ice pop sticks or reusable ice pop tops with attached sticks. Let the pops freeze for at least 24 hours.

5. To unmold the pops, see page 16.

THE CREAMSICLE

Who didn't love eating those super-sweet orange push-pops when they were growing up? I know I was a huge fan and seriously hated it when I reached the bottom of the treat. This version is definitely not as sweet as those summer desserts (probably a good thing), but the color and creamy texture will definitely take you on a trip down memory lane. Except this time you're old enough to drive a car, vote, and purchase the orange vodka you need to spike the pops.

¾ cup prepared orange vodka (page 10)

¼ cup prepared triple sec (page 10)

1¼ cups orange juice, preferably freshly squeezed

¼ cup heavy cream

2 tablespoons sugar

1. Prepare and chill the orange vodka and triple sec of your choice.

2. In a medium bowl, combine the orange vodka, triple sec, orange juice, heavy cream, and sugar.

3. Carefully divide the mixture equally among your ice pop molds. Do not fill the molds to the top. Leave a small amount of space to allow for expansion when the liquid freezes.

4. Top with ice pop sticks or reusable ice pop tops with attached sticks. Let the pops freeze for at least 24 hours.

5. To unmold the pops, see page 16.

COQUITO

Coquito is a Puerto Rican version of eggnog, and it is rich and very boozy. If you take a few minutes to look up "coquito" online, you'll find an amusing array of variations. Some are made with eggs, some without, and many are accompanied by sweeping proclamations declaring that it is the true and authentic version. My boyfriend's mother, Annette, graciously shared her personal recipe for this decadent treat with me. She uses raw eggs (both whipped whites and yolks), and while I don't have a problem with that and happily drink my glass down to the very bottom with a big smile of delight on my face, I know raw egg freaks a lot of people out, so I've altered the Poptail version accordingly. It's still Annette's coquito—in spirit at least.

1 cup prepared white rum (page 10)

⅓ cup evaporated milk

⅓ cup sweetened condensed milk

½ cup cream of coconut

⅓ cup whole milk

1 teaspoon vanilla extract

½ teaspoon ground cinnamon

¼ teaspoon ground nutmeg

1. Prepare and chill the white rum of your choice.

2. In a medium bowl, combine the white rum, evaporated milk, sweetened condensed milk, cream of coconut, whole milk, vanilla extract, cinnamon, and nutmeg.

3. Carefully divide the mixture equally among your ice pop molds. Do not fill the molds to the top. Leave a small amount of space to allow for expansion when the liquid freezes.

4. Top with ice pop sticks or reusable ice pop tops with attached sticks. Let the pops freeze for at least 24 hours.

5. To unmold the pops, see page 16.

CHAPTER EIGHT

DESSERT ON A STICK

OATMEAL COOKIE

This pop wins the award for most likely to cause a stampede, and the coveted title of most likely to make your guests exclaim things like, "I'm in love!" and "It tastes just like a cookie! How is this possible?!" Plus you now have an excuse to buy a sparkly bottle of gold-flecked cinnamon schnapps at your local liquor store. When the clerk looks at you with raised eyebrows, simply flash him a big smile and confidently tell them that it's for a very important recipe.

¾ cup prepared Baileys Irish Cream (page 10)

½ cup prepared butterscotch schnapps (page 10)

½ cup prepared gold-flecked cinnamon schnapps (page 10)

¾ cup heavy cream

1. Prepare and chill the Baileys Irish Cream, butterscotch schnapps, and cinnamon schnapps.

2. In a medium bowl, combine the Irish cream, butterscotch and cinnamon schnapps, and heavy cream.

3. Carefully divide the mixture equally among your ice pop molds. Do not fill the molds to the top. Leave a small amount of space to allow for expansion when the liquid freezes.

4. Top with ice pop sticks or reusable ice pop tops with attached sticks. Let the pops freeze for at least 24 hours.

5. To unmold the pops, see page 16.

BIG GIRL ROOT BEER FLOAT

Root beer schnapps is something that actually exists. However, like a unicorn, it can sometimes be very hard to find. If you aren't able to locate this type of liqueur, you can substitute vanilla vodka for an equally pleasing pop experience.

¾ cup prepared root beer schnapps or vanilla vodka (page 10)

1½ cups flattened root beer (page 12)

¼ cup heavy cream

1. Prepare and chill the root beer schnapps or vodka of your choice, and let the root beer flatten for at least 8 hours.

2. In a medium bowl, combine the root beer schnapps or vodka, root beer, and heavy cream.

3. Carefully divide the mixture equally among your ice pop molds. Do not fill the molds to the top. Leave a small amount of space to allow for expansion when the liquid freezes.

4. Top with ice pop sticks or reusable ice pop tops with attached sticks. Let the pops freeze for at least 24 hours.

5. To unmold the pops, see page 16.

BANANA SPLIT

Cherries? Check! Bananas? Check! Whipped cream? Check and check! The only thing missing is ice cream, but since we're freezing this decadent concoction of liqueur and fruit together, I truly believe we've covered all of the bases in this frozen treat.

¾ cup prepared banana liqueur (page 10)

¼ cup prepared whipped cream vodka (page 10)

1 cup banana cream yogurt

¼ cup finely diced banana

¼ cup quartered maraschino cherries

1. Prepare and chill the banana liqueur and whipped cream vodka of your choice.

2. In a medium bowl, combine the banana liqueur, whipped cream vodka, banana cream yogurt, diced banana, and maraschino cherries.

3. Carefully divide the mixture equally among your ice pop molds. Do not fill the molds to the top. Leave a small amount of space to allow for expansion when the liquid freezes.

4. Top with ice pop sticks or reusable ice pop tops with attached sticks. Let the pops freeze for at least 24 hours.

5. To unmold the pops, see page 16.

THE PUMPKIN PATCH

In terms of fun flavors, I am absolutely gaga over this pumpkin-spiked pop.
It's perfect for a grown-up Halloween bash or as a funky Thanksgiving
dessert. After all, pie is so 2011. Definitely take the time to hunt down a
container of pumpkin juice so you can see what all the fuss is about.

   1 cup prepared dark spiced rum (page 10)

   1½ cups pumpkin juice, such as Odwalla Pumpkin Protein

   1 teaspoon ground cinnamon

   1½ teaspoons vanilla extract

1. Prepare and chill the spiced rum of your choice.

2. In a medium bowl, combine the spiced rum, pumpkin juice, cinnamon, and
   vanilla extract.

3. Carefully divide the mixture equally among your ice pop molds. Do not fill
   the molds to the top. Leave a small amount of space to allow for expansion
   when the liquid freezes.

4. Top with ice pop sticks or reusable ice pop tops with attached sticks. Let the
   pops freeze for at least 24 hours.

5. To unmold the pops, see page 16.

MOM'S APPLE PIE

A few years ago when the craze for alcohol that's flavored like candy and baked goods erupted, I was against the whole thing. Whipped cream vodka? Give me a break. Of course, eventually I caved and tried some, and it was seriously scrumptious. Don't worry; I'm over my attitude now, as super-sweet booze has allowed me to make ice pops that taste like apple pie filling.

> 1 cup prepared whipped cream vodka (page 10)
>
> ¼ cup simple syrup (page 14)
>
> 1¼ cups apple cider

1. Prepare and chill the whipped cream vodka of your choice and the simple syrup.

2. In a medium bowl, combine the whipped cream vodka, simple syrup, and apple cider.

3. Carefully divide the mixture equally among your ice pop molds. Do not fill the molds to the top. Leave a small amount of space to allow for expansion when the liquid freezes.

4. Top with ice pop sticks or reusable ice pop tops with attached sticks. Let the pops freeze for at least 24 hours.

5. To unmold the pops, see page 16.

GERMAN CHOCOLATE CAKE

An ice pop that tastes like cake? Yes, please! You probably think I'm exaggerating, but this array of liquors and heavy cream somehow magically transcends space and time to create an ice-cold slice of German chocolate cake—no beaters, eggs, or painstakingly iced layers.

¾ cup prepared coconut rum (page 10)

¾ cup prepared crème de cacao (page 10)

¾ cup prepared hazelnut liqueur, such as Frangelicio (page 10)

¼ cup heavy cream

¼ cup shredded sweetened coconut, divided

1. Prepare and chill the coconut rum, crème de cacao, and hazelnut liqueur of your choice.

2. In a medium bowl, combine the three liquors and the heavy cream. Divide half of the sweetened coconut among your ice pop molds.

3. Carefully divide the liquid mixture equally among your ice pop molds, pouring it over the coconut. Do not fill the molds to the top. Leave a small amount of space to allow for expansion when the liquid freezes.

4. Sprinkle the remaining shredded coconut into the molds, dividing it evenly, and then top with ice pop sticks or reusable ice pop tops with attached sticks. Let the pops freeze for at least 24 hours.

5. To unmold the pops, see page 16.

CARROT CAKE

The ground cinnamon in this recipe tends to pool at the top of the pop. As I developed the pops, I found that I liked this effect (it gave them sort of a warm ombre-colored tip). It's especially fetching when you're using molds shaped like stars or rockets. However, if you do not particularly enjoy a burst of cinnamon, you can certainly elect to leave it out or use a cinnamon-flavored extract in its place.

> 1 cup prepared spiced rum or dark rum (page 10)
>
> ½ cup brown sugar simple syrup (page 15)
>
> 1 cup carrot juice, such as Bolthouse Farms
>
> 1 teaspoon ground cinnamon
>
> 1½ teaspoons vanilla extract

1. Prepare and chill the spiced rum of your choice and the brown sugar simple syrup.

2. In a medium bowl, combine the rum, brown sugar simple syrup, carrot juice, cinnamon, and vanilla extract.

3. Carefully divide the mixture equally among your ice pop molds. Do not fill the molds to the top. Leave a small amount of space to allow for expansion when the liquid freezes.

4. Top with ice pop sticks or reusable ice pop tops with attached sticks. Let the pops freeze for at least 24 hours.

5. To unmold the pops, see page 16.

CHERRY CHEESECAKE

Cheesecake-flavored pudding is a magical concoction that is not only delicious but also comes in sugar-free and therefore guilt-free varieties. Layer it with a fat-free cherry yogurt and you've practically made health food. We'll just pretend that those pesky alcohol calories don't count. Deal?

¾ cup prepared cherry vodka (page 10)

¼ cup prepared whipped cream vodka (page 10)

1 cup cherry yogurt

½ cup cheesecake-flavored pudding

1. Prepare and chill the cherry and whipped cream vodkas of your choice.

2. In a medium bowl, combine the cherry and whipped cream vodkas, cherry yogurt, and cheesecake-flavored pudding.

3. Carefully divide the mixture equally among your ice pop molds. Do not fill the molds to the top. Leave a small amount of space to allow for expansion when the liquid freezes.

4. Top with ice pop sticks or reusable ice pop tops with attached sticks. Let the pops freeze for at least 24 hours.

5. To unmold the pops, see page 16.

Conversions

MEASURE	EQUIVALENT	METRIC
1 teaspoon	--	5 milliliters
1 tablespoon	3 teaspoons	14.8 milliliters
1 cup	16 tablespoons	236.8 milliliters
1 pint	2 cups	473.6 milliliters
1 quart	4 cups	947.2 milliliters
1 liter	4 cups + 3½ tablespoons	1000 milliliters
1 ounce (dry)	2 tablespoons	28.35 grams
1 pound	16 ounces	453.49 grams
2.21 pounds	35.3 ounces	1 kilogram
325°F/350°F/375°F	--	165°C/177°C/190°C

Acknowledgments

Many thanks to my trusty pop brigade who graciously volunteered to taste my concoctions, even the bizarre ones: Pam Aghababian, Stephanie Belbusti, Kristen Bourgault, Emma Heffern, and Meghan Lorina.

A tremendous round of applause to Anna Diaz and Hänni Baatz, who agreed to read and reread everything I wrote and gave thoughtful yet kind feedback.

And a special infinity of x's and o's to CK for putting up with my turning our wee city kitchen into a veritable ice pop speakeasy for months and months.